MEL BAY PRESENTS

El McMeen

SOLO GUITAR SERENADE

A recording of the music in this book is now available. The publisher strongly recommends the use of this recording along with the text to insure accuracy of interpretation and ease in learning.

CONTENTS

NOTE TO READERS
REGARDING CGDGAD TUNING

All the arrangements in this volume are played in CGDGAD tuning. I learned this tuning from the music of Dave Evans, an excellent British guitar player, and it has become "standard" to me. I now play everything in this tuning (with an occasional foray into DADGAD).

If you are not familiar with this tuning, do not lose heart or panic: it is magnificent! The ease of playing, the sonority of the instrument, the suspensions and over-tones—all of these and many other attributes will make your playing memorable to listeners as you become familiar with CGDGAD.

My arrangements in this tuning are contained in many other Mel Bay books, in-cluding the following:

Of Soul and Spirit
Irish Guitar Encores
The Complete Celtic Fingerstyle Guitar Book
New Dimensions and Explorations for Fingerstyle Guitar

In addition, for systematic instruction, you may be interested in my video guitar lessons for Stefan Grossman's Guitar Workshop, P.O. Box 802, Sparta, NJ 07871, covering traditional Irish music, Christmas songs and sacred music generally. Those video lessons utilize sophisticated split-screen techniques. If you have any questions or suggestions, please feel free to contact me either through Mel Bay Publications or directly c/o Piney Ridge Music, P.O. Box 73, Mtn. Lakes, NJ 07046.

El McMeen

WHEN YOU AND I WERE YOUNG, MAGGIE

My wife loves this poignant song by George W. Johnson about the death of Johnson's wife within one year of their marriage in 1865.

WHEN YOU AND I WERE YOUNG, MAGGIE

Tuning : C G D G A D
Capo : V

*This page has been
left blank to avoid
awkward page turns*

FANNY POWER

This beautiful melody is by legendary blind Irish harper Turlough O'Carolan (1670–1738). Fanny Power, incidentally, was the daughter of Mrs. Power, for whom "Carolan's Concerto" was composed.

FANNY POWER

Tuning: C G D G A D **A**

Trad. Arr. El McMeen

STAR OF THE COUNTY DOWN

I credit a guitar friend from Moline, Illinois, Jerry Schroeder, with giving me the idea for this arrangement.

STAR OF THE COUNTY DOWN

Tuning : C G D G A D
Capo : IV

Introduction

This page has been left blank to avoid awkward page turns

ASHOKAN FAREWELL

This is the great tune by fiddler Jay Ungar that many people associate with the *Civil War* series on PBS. It is an original composition, but sounds traditional.

ASHOKAN FAREWELL
(By JAY UNGAR)

Tuning : C G D G A D
Capo : II

JOCK O'HAZELDEAN

This arrangement was inspired by Martin Simpson's playing of this song.

JOCK O'HAZELDEAN

Tuning: C G D G A D

Trad. Arr. El McMeen

CAROLAN'S DREAM

This is not actually a Carolan tune, but was composed by Thomas Connellan under the title "Molly MacAlpin."

CAROLAN'S DREAM

Tuning : C G D G A D
Capo   : II

Arrangement © 1994 El McMeen's Piney Ridge Music.

SHEEBEG AND SHEEMORE; CAROLAN'S WELCOME

Two great Carolan tunes, "Sheebeg" is in the key of C, and "Welcome" in the key of G minor, each capoed up.

SHEEBEG AND SHEEMORE

Tuning : C G D G A D
Capo   : II

* Return to part A; take second ending.

*This page has been
left blank to avoid
awkward page turns*

CAROLAN'S WELCOME

Tuning : C G D G A D
Capo : II

OUR GOD, OUR HELP / IMMORTAL, INVISIBLE

The full titles of these powerful hymns are, of course, "Our God, Our Help in Ages Past" (W. Croft) and "Immortal, Invisible, God Only Wise" (Welsh hymn melody).

OUR GOD, OUR HELP IN AGES PAST

Tuning : C G D G A D
Capo : II

IMMORTAL, INVISIBLE, GOD ONLY WISE

Tuning : C G D G A D
Capo : II

Arrangement © 1994 El McMeen's Piney Ridge Music.

SKYE BOAT SONG / I RIDE AN OLD PAINT

A medley of the beautiful lullaby about Bonny Prince Charlie, and the lonesome night-herding cowboy tune.

SKYE BOAT SONG

Tuning : C G D G A D
Capo   : IV

*This page has been
left blank to avoid
awkward page turns*

I RIDE AN OLD PAINT

Tuning : C G D G A D
Capo   : IV